THE
SHORTEST
DISTANCE

poems by Kathleen Thompson

The
Shortest
Distance

poems by Kathleen Thompson

Published by
COOSA RIVER BOOKS
368 Sugar Loaf Hill Road
Deatsville, Alabama 36022

Library of Congress Control Number: 2008909542
ISBN: 978-0-9785401-2-8
Cover Art by Carolyn Watson
Printed in the United States

Also by Kathleen Thompson

Searching for Ambergris

The Nights, The Days

Acknowledgements

The author gratefully acknowledges the following publications in which these poems have appeared:

Amaryllis: "Men Going Fishing," "Neighbor," "Lament," "The Shortest Distance," "In the Sweet, By and By"
Bellowing Ark: "Beauty and Distance"
Birmingham Poetry Review: "Sisters"
Georgia Journal: "Inertia"
New Laurel Review: "Fruits of an Age"
Oracle: "The Radius of a Wave"
Oktoberfest IV: "Quick Agony"
Savannah Literary Review: "Men Who Buy Lunch at the Pig," "The Last Page"
Sou'wester: "Fusion," "Women Fleeing Ice"
Spanish Moss: "Eating Dirt" (version called "Family Dirt")
The Journal of the Georgia State Medical Association: "Possessions"
The Georgia Guardian: "Emma's Song"
Thicket: "As They Wait," "Kitchen Psalter"
Valley Planet: "Icon"

"Woman's Wait" was first published in *When The Wind Stops*, a Desert Storm anthology edited by Laura Sargent. "Men Going Fishing" was chosen for *Whatever Remembers Us: An Alabama Anthology* edited by Sue Brannan Walker and J. William Chambers. Thanks for this historic effort.

"Men Going Fishing," "November Kitchen," "My Back Porch, November," "Woman's Wait," "Lament," "The Shortest Distance," "In the Sweet, By and By," "Fruits of an Age," and "Women Fleeing Ice" were published in a chapbook, *Searching for Ambergris*. Thanks to Jennifer Bosveld, editor, Pudding House Publications.

Several poems, sometimes in earlier versions, have received awards from The Poetry Society of Georgia and the Alabama State Poetry Society. I am grateful to those organizations for their support of my poetry over many years.

"The Radius of a Wave" won the First Place 2004 Vivian Smallwood Award at the Eugene Walter Writers Festival sponsored by the University of South Alabama.

"Eating Dirt" was a finalist in the Nineteenth Annual Ann Stanford Poetry Prize, Spring 2008.

"The Shortest Distance" won the Cosmos Mariner Award sponsored by The Poetry Society of Georgia.

I am indebted most to my family—Tommy, Teresa, Tracy—for their unconditional support of all my writing, but especially to Stephen, my business partner, first and final reader of my poems, my muse—my son. His bulldog persistence and his poetic sensibilities were both invaluable in this project. Too, I am grateful for my grandchildren, Nicholas and Victoria, *xoxo*, whose very being raises the emotional bar of my writing in all genres.

And following that, I salute my generous and forever friend, Carolyn Watson, for the cover art. Her ability to wed the visual and the tactile with the written image remains, in spite of adversity, as well as her great good humor. Thanks, good buddy.

I am deeply grateful to my editor, Susan Shehane, whose heart is stellar, and whose prose has a lyrical grace of its own, no doubt informed by the musical line. As a teacher and publisher, she works tirelessly to support other Alabama writers, a rare and worthy trait. Without her enthusiasm for my poems and her encouragement, this dream might never have become a reality.

I am humbled and honored by the affirmation of Nelle Harper Lee, who, after first reading my chapbook of poems, wanted more. And so, it has come to pass.

To the fistful of poets in the charter class of Spalding University's MFA in Writing program, and to our mentor, Greg Pape, thank you. It was in that program that I learned to write both poetry and fiction, again and again. Thanks also to Director Sena Jeter Naslund whose work led me there in the first place and who continues to inspire me; and to Karen Mann, her able assistant in founding the program.

Finally, I thank each friend in the universe upon whom I have inflicted every conceivable poetic effort: drafts, poems old enough to have beards, maimed poems, failed poems, pitiful poems, revised poems, exercise and practice poems, poems that weren't poems—and for yet abiding me.

The author also wishes to acknowledge the work of:
Carl Michael Bellman

> *1740–95, Swedish poet; protégé of Gustavus III. His early poetry was chiefly religious. His dithyrambic odes in Fredmans Epistlar (1790) and Fredmans Sånger (1791) include bacchanals, pastorals, and comic pieces. A fine performer of his own verse, Bellman sometimes wrote music for it, but more often he borrowed French melodies and music from contemporary plays.*
>
> *–The Columbia Encyclopedia, Sixth Edition, 2001-05.*

On a trip to Sweden in May, 1981, my husband and I were entertained by a group of business men who took us to dinner in a restaurant just off a narrow street in the oldest district of Stockholm. When they learned I was a writer, they began to sing praises for one whose work they loved, C. M. Bellman. Later one of them mailed me a 33 1/3 record, "To Carl Michael with Love," of Bellman's songs translated by Paul Britten Austin and performed by Martin Best Consort. My memory of these haunting lyrics has outlasted the technology with which they were recorded.

Contents

For Tommy

Woman's Wait

Sleep, sweet tiny Carl, in peace,
"Twill soon be time to wake thee;
Time to taste our time's disease,
Whose bile shall ne'er forsake thee.

-C. M. Bellman, "Cradle Song,"
translated by Paul Britten Austin

Pole Yard at Brownville

Naked poles stacked in rows
the way sausages are shown,
or long skinny bolognas

scraped clean of the nubby skin
and knots by men whose shaved
faces felt like buttered leather

but whose cracks in the hands
might stain a yellow dotted Swiss
dress, or snag a grosgrain ribbon

so maybe that's why Daddy didn't
hug me when I asked how I looked
dressed to walk to Sunday School,

but stood back and let his eyes
take in Mama's clean handiwork.
"Beauty is as beauty does."

Other stacks were blackest black,
already processed and stained
by vats of creosote exuding an odor

as distinctive as a chocolate bar
of Baby Ruth at the commissary
when the whistle blew four o'clock.

Ole '97's whistle is what I waited
for as it chugged on down to Buhl.
As I tittered on one of its tracks,

I wondered how long I could balance
myself, how far I could follow the train
away from this wooded red valley.

Quick Agony

No matter.
It is only a mill house
scorched and blackened
like the poles
on the wood yard
and the men
who peel them.
It isn't even
on the hill
but across the tracks
close to the quarters.
The superintendent
barks for buckets
above the crashes
of charred beams.
As the fatwood-fed
flames jump and hiss,
the crane operator
spits tobacco juice
over his shoulder
outside the circle
of spectators.

He grumbles how the wife
allowed she'd burn the Christmas pine
before the four o'clock whistle,
before the bad luck of tomorrow,
New Year's, and how she'd crammed
a limb into the heater right nigh
to an hour after she'd added
the scuttle of coal.
She hunches nearby
holding a balding china doll,
twisting its empty
paisley sleeve.
No matter.
It is a fast fire.

Inertia

The eye of my storm encircles me
while spring urgency swirls within,
as surprising a reversal
as the first who shall be last.

Chores churn to head the list:
sweep winter cobwebs,
paint rooms,
change wallpaper,
clean closets. . .

Yet nothing has moved
except the cherry blossom
drifting onto my arm
as I stand near
the March madness
of washed-on color strips,
and like the wistful
weight of wisteria,
the blossom
holds me still.

Putting in Plumbago
for Lettye

Swapping plants and plant talk
around the privacy fence
that separates our back yards
links me to my neighbor.
She offers graciously;
I accept greedily,
hungry for her blossoms.

Their pale blue promise
mocks the September rusts
and oranges of my new bed
of sturdy coxcombs, and mums;
these dare to dance on frilly stems,
infusive, she says, clipping,
pulling hard to get some roots.

She thinks of the disease first,
calls its name, and wonders
if I might like some Queen Anne's Lace
taking over the place, everywhere,
and after both are in my ground,
she reaches up to snatch out
a strand of dead jasmine,

intertwined on our common wall,
pruned and made manageable
just last week and now *look at it already*;
she tucks a vagrant tendril into place
as we start back inside to disparate
lives; her need to clip and shape;
mine to infuse, infuse.

Names

In Memoriam: Tempie Savannah Taylor Smith
November 18, 1902 – September 28, 1966

Her name was Ella,
Violia Hasslentine Ella
Sanford Taylor.
I never saw her chop cotton
or cabbage for kraut.
I never heard her hum
the lyrics yellowing now
in her trunk for one
of their seventeen.

I never saw the bundling
board , or the dog trot,
but fireplace rocks still
stand there, outwitting time
like a marble monument
marking hours spent
stirring syrup and stews
and nurturing new names.

She named you Savannah.
Had she felt the spiky
side of a sand dollar?
Had she ever chased
a bevy of sand pipers?
Did the breeze that bends
sea oats cause her to shiver
as she stoked the fire?

You never saw that place
she conjured up for you.
You named me Mary Kathleen,
youngest of twelve. My pew
in Savannah is marked with brass:
I sit next to your shiny name
and wonder what you dreamed
for me—what horizons, what sea?

En Route: Savannah to Aiken

Steepled clapboard snuggling
next to live oaks that drip
lazy moss near ponds
padded with flat lilies,
white on green, a docile
scene repeated every
twenty miles or so.

Women named these churches.
Otherwise locations
might have mattered;
names of saints, surfaced.

Instead, First Thankful,
Higher Ground, Mt. Joy—
names that sing that chorus
like goldenrod, pervading
every unattended inch
of earth. Abounding.
Unabased. Unending.

Woman's Wait

...believing in old men's lies
                    -Ezra Pound

I have given up passion
for Lent, thinking
of boys
who fight our wars
conceived by men.
What do boys know
of this war
that Saddam Hussein started,
of desert dwellers they protect?
Women know wars,
have nursed all boys.
Last August
when a black ship
filled two wall-sized windows
overlooking Savannah River,
mothers, sweethearts,
and wives waved and shouted
to the boys on deck,
and I waved, too,
moved by the moment.
In another war
Obie's mother waited
at the Waynesboro Station
and fainted
when she heard the whistle
of the train
bearing from France
Obie's remains.
I wait on this war
wearing ashes
for those who won't.

The Least of These

Stones stretch out of sight,
mortared into a mosaic path,
as hot in July as a wood-fired oven.
The opulence of Rubins and Raphael,
Bernini, and Botticelli have blunted
my vision—angels with the Madonna
and Child, the Sistine ceiling hands,
tapestries of the papal apartments.
Fuzzy-eyed with heat and history,
I try to resist this woman's plea.

She is folded in half,
her back flung forward,
limp, creased by poverty,
haphazard origami
mummified in rags,
as tortured as the faces
of gargoyles above
a narrow *via* in a *piazza*
of raucous pigeons.
She strains upward like Adam
toward tourists circling
the Vatican walls, as fixed
on reaching St. Peter's bones,
and Michelangelo's *Pieta*
as the hands of a Swiss clock.
Hell-bent on rounding the corners
and finding the door to go in
for a glimpse, a postcard perhaps
of the *Virgin Mary and Jesus,*
they ignore her outstretched tin cup,
its single coin rattling like death.

If I Had A Hussif

If I had a hussif—
one of plain cloth, maybe wool—
not beaded nor embroidered,
I could save this news
like a broken button
and cram it into a substantial
pocket, along with the tears
in the eyes of our children,
the caution in your doctor's
and the terror in yours.

Or fold it with crisp creases
the way of men's handkerchiefs,
defined, like their fears, and dry.
Columbus must have had one,
gone from home so long,
and he must have considered
along with his essential mending,
must have flinched at least,
at sunset, over the *what ifs*
and *wherefores* of that looming edge.

The Civil War soldier, too,
contemplating his sorry plight,
cringing at each bloody face
after he fired his close-up shot,
fearing a face too familiar,
a face with his own features,
wishing for their mother now
to patch up their great squabble,
and their wounds, wishing for his wife
to darn so many gaping holes.

The threads of my life,
not separately seamed,
bleed into a tie-dyed whole,
so if I had a hussif, perhaps
I would not cry over jonquils,
their early coming and going,
nor the obituary of a stranger,
nor your single sock
lost somewhere
during the wash.

hussif: variation of housewife, *huswif;* a small case for sewing.

Examples of a *hussif* are on display at the Ships of the Sea Museum in Savannah, and at the Museum of the Confederacy in New Orleans.

Beauty and Distance

Slim white stem of egret
skims over cord grass,
slows, descends for fishing;

perches—breath-catching snowy
mound, two feet high, on reed thin
stilted legs—startles, strokes through air,

settles atop a distant cypress;
neck stretched high, an angel
posing, ornamental, ethereal again.

Lament
for Ivodean

If we had simply walked the sands
of Seacrest an hour earlier this morning

before the emerald water was pinked
and skirted with foamy frilly-edged waves;

if the sea turtle had swum that great seaway
more slowly, if the undertow had been stronger,

tugging her away from her destined stop
just below the line of peat and sea oats;

if her lumbering, laboring steps through sand
had been less straight, less determined;

then we might have seen her begin the dig,
might have observed the high drama of that act,

its flawless timing, her eyes locked ahead
as the first contraction hit, an egg dropped out

until one hundred or so were safely covered
to foil hungry seagulls and sand pipers

crazed at the notion of eggs, eggs,
eggshells under such staggering weight,

a paradox we might have witnessed up close,
forgetting our complex pains, watching hers.

Son Slipping Away

What's our world? An isle of woe!
Breathing, born, to death we go;
Too soon the grave will take thee.

-C. M. Bellman, "Cradle Song,"
translated by Paul Britten Austin

Los Niños

She wore a portable chest,
necklace for a neck so slim
it might be strangled
by this weight of styrofoam.
An apparition staring up at us,
splattering penury like raindrops
against the thin windshield.

We waited for an armed signal,
slow-motion permission
from these men with guns
to enter and pass through
their land of dirt floors,
and foreign *r*'s.

She eased the lid open
to a large crack,
then snapped it down,
tender temptress baring herself,
seduction of blood sausages,
drawn up and stacked
like bones or sticks.

Here, cactuses as old as the ruins,
whose sprawling gray-green limbs
will not fit the frame of a photograph
and children begging in a language
tourists are warned against.
Here, barefoot, in San Ignacio,
they welcomed our van, waving wares,
stalks of wilted staghorn ferns.

At the *Cataratas dos Iguaçu,*
another *vendedora* , less sure
of herself, plies her whispers
around a museum display,
her family outside, the Guarani,
whittling *coti mundis* and crocodiles
with craggy backs or braiding
bright belts and bracelets,

as compelling as one of my own children
drawing me aside from a crowd
to share some secret, a sound
recognizable to a mother
like her baby's first whimpers for milk,
inciting her breasts
to dampness.

At first there was no face
and then when there was,
I had to turn mine, to look outside
past lush red hibiscus, blue plumbago,
and purple agapanthus lilies to water
spilling over in two countries,
for she had nothing to offer,
no greenery, no goods,
just the tiniest of urgings,

and I looked to the water falls,
so wide they fooled my eyes.
Yes, I turned my head, looked away
for I feared a rush rivaling
the raging waters of these many rivers
culminating in the shape of a horseshoe
at the throat of the devil, *Garganta Diablo,*
thirsty and gulping torrents of water,
I feared falling myself...

soaked by that inevitable spray.
I shiver, a continent away
as I arrange photos of sacred ruins
where Jesuits once rose at four
to pray for the heathen natives,
to apprise them of sin,
and to sip on their morning *maté*.

No *maté* for me.
Papel hygiénico was the blessing
I sought outside these fallen walls
at the rustic toilet. That one,
the boy with hungry eyes,
was keeper of the cup of coins
guardian of his half-empty roll.
His eyes dogged mine,
as I rifled through my purse,
frantic, half-blinded by the sun.

I feel it all clearly now,
as sleet sheets my window,
his skimpy enterprise, and theirs,
the zoom lens of distance
burning in the imprint
of their wishful voices,
those little toes, stubby
and brown, *sin* shoes.

Cataratas dos Iguaçu: It is said that when Eleanor Roosevelt first saw these immense waterfalls at Iguaçu, she proclaimed, "Poor Victoria."

Garganta Diablo, throat of the devil. This is the point at which many rivers converge and culminate into one huge, horse-shaped set of falls.

The Move

1

The lap dog snaps, begging
and untrained but fully fed, nips
at the toes of the grandmother.
She lacks the words to say,
writing in the quiet of night.
She snuggles him in her lap
as she tries again to order
daylight things, storing spices,
arranging pots, dreams dreamed
for her daughter, as fragile
as the box of crystal, shattered
underneath a lingerie chest.

2

You breaked my dream,
the five year old complains,
awakened in his new room.
Nightly he clicks primary colors,
matching holes in Legos,
assembling, joining, creating
out of a pile of chaos a thing
colorful and useful, vehicle
to travel back to his old room.
His great-grandmother helped paint
it as blue as the sky on their cul-de-sac
next to Cactus Mountain, claimed
and named by him and his Papa.
There cactuses had no thorns,
and toys were not stacked
and stored in plastic boxes.

Clicking again, he changes the shape
to a weapon, something destructive,
to ward off the enemy, invisible,
hiding among cardboard boxes
in this new cramped place
with only a path cleared to pass.

He sleeps with his plastic blocks,
hides them in his school bag.
He cannot be without them.
They change to suit his needs,
a mirror of grownups around him.
That last day he tells his friends
how to find his new home, how close
it will be to his school. They stare
at him with vacant eyes. Where
will he ride his bike, they wonder.
Will he have a creek with earthworms
slithering in the slimy moss?
Will he ever come back?

Clicking again. He sorts out
a good guy who might save Mommy.
She rips open boxes looking for towels
she knows she packed somewhere,
sobs when a light bulb breaks.
What box is his dog book in?
Did it go into storage
or with his daddy?

Now a symmetrical castle rises smoothly,
tall and perfectly formed, slick and blue,
with no misplaced toys, no gargoyles,
a place for mommies and daddies
and babies and pets to live inside,
happily ever after.

3

His mother scrubs grime
from the corners of kitchen cabinets,
overlooked by happier cooks
serving up contented suppers,

grinds her knuckles red
with disinfectant and bleach,
toothbrushes grout
mildewed above the tub.
Unacceptable
          as is another person's dirt,
          as was another woman.
What smudges won't budge
she whitens with paint,
even inside the linen closet.
She sweeps cobwebs from corners,
scours sinks, cleaning these rented
rooms, settling them into order,
a paradigm for her splintered heart.

The Shortest Distance
for Nicholas, at seven

Angles with formulas over equations,
axioms memorized over the unknowns;
earliest choices so easily concluded.

Now as we meander along this rickrack
of shoreline, our tracks skirting the water,
we pore over shells being swallowed

into wet sandy graves; we pick one up
and try to thumb him open, as tightly seamed
as a green pistachio, then throw him back;

we scan the drier sand for fresh turtle tracks
and follow the smooth slide to a roped-off
orange square dated by a tracker today.

The wind will sweep her mounds level,
disguise the high drama of timing her dig,
of her great effort to release the eggs,

her eyes locked in a glazed-over stare
each time a contraction begins and ends
with another of the one hundred eggs laid.

This part I will not explain to you now.
Anyhow, you will be spared that one pain.
I run back to the surf and walk backwards,

an old Indian trick, I tell you, but you know that one
already, so we grab the bucket near our umbrella,
to start an aquarium with seaweed and water.

We each net the waves crashing onto sand
in threes; yours is squirming with a sand flea,
a baby flounder, and minnows of all sizes

while mine hangs empty; I am dawdling
unable to stay on task with this strange
arithmetic that at once suspends time

and yet has it speeding away, a catamaran,
sails puffed, grown miniscule, the size
of little hands spread in plaster, as fast

as your mother and her brother grew
too shy to hold mine, too busy for sand castles.
Factor in this constant of passing time

and the shortest distance between two points
is not always the straightest line; the brown
mermaid's purse lies emptied, curled up;

the spidery hermit crab lurks inside a shell;
the turtle tracks will be erased. Our hyperbolic
beach mornings burn away long before noon.

The Radius of a Wave
for Nicholas at eight

1
He boards the thin dragon skimmer
to practice at the ragged edge,
egg-shaped, as fast as its red fire—
if the water catches under it,

if he jumps on it with both feet,
if he balances with his arms,
he will skim over the sand,
as free as a seagull feather

loosed, unaware yet of hair,
of combs and mirrors and hats,
unabashed at what parents wear.
His mother sand sculpts a Stitch.

He floats his boogie board out
and takes the top of a figure eight,
riding its highest curl to the crash,
then floats back out again.

Up and over, curling under, crashing,
the wave flattens and foams on the sand,
the upper half of a circumference;
his goggles duck under the curve

then surface again. Another starts
its upward climb and he is ready.
Ready for the radius—no more
wading in the foam and wishing,

no more standing to net the waves
with me, no more clinging hard
onto my eager hand. He bounds out
into the deeper water with his Papa.

2
Early mornings he is younger
and we search for shells. I'm
content only with unbroken bivalves,
but he looks for the twisty ones,

any surviving parts will do:
he can see the whole gastropod,
imagine it added to his collection.
He tries to teach me selectivity

as I skip bony, broken shards,
unwilling to risk filling my cup
by choosing them before I spot
the flawless ones. Confident,

he fills his bucket with keepers.
Two girls giggle by with boogie
boards. He shoves his shells to me
and distances himself with a little jog.

The girls slow down and run out
to take a wave. He smoothes his hair
and retrieves a board that's floated away.
I hold my breath as he dives under deep.

Distant Vigil
for Nicholas at nine

The silence here in August
drones out summer's games
when one yell of *Marco* echoed
a ring of multiple *Polo's*, a pool
of squeals and slaps of water
as they flounced and chased
like frog fish.

Invisible in the shade,
I glanced up from my page,
heart stopped
until his goggled head
emerged. My fear
of deep water cascading,
I made myself known,
grandmother, lifeguard,
listen to me.

Our eyes met sometimes,
his need for my distant vigil,
mine, to seine for signs of peril.
Such quiet makes me wonder
what minnow eyes school him
this first week in fourth grade,
whether they know yet
the murky depths.

Chance
for Nicholas at ten

Then let not winter's ragged hand deface
In thee thy summer ere thou be distill'd...
Ten times thyself were happier than thou art,
If ten of thine ten times refigur'd be.
  Sonnet VI William Shakespeare

Tens are essential
in "Around the World."
Shake the cup; blow
luck on five hot die.
Fives are fifty, you say;
one is one hundred.
Triples are worth more:
three ones, a thousand.
In between is nothing,
busted, lose your turn.

Better to lose a turn
than a knot of friendship
in the Super Chevron pattern
or to cut the embroidery thread
too short for the Braided Buddy.
We both prefer a less tedious design,
doubling five different colored
strands, knotting an end, twisting
the ten and letting go to see it
crinkle into a Sweet Twisty bracelet.

Better still than to miss a girl
gone from the pool for a week.
You cut the cards for gin rummy,
but you ask about my first crush.
I deal the cards, turn up his name,

but decline to divulge more,
resist warning you against caring,
the challenging nature of it,
what comes between the *tens*,
those errant parameters of love.

Repetition
for Nicholas at eleven

The school puberty video
and its accompanying
toothpaste, deodorant,
and small booklet
of such importance
you must secret it from the bag
occurred on the same day
you asked about *haiku*
homework and alliteration.

Three very short lines
of seventeen syllables
are limited by
your four-syllable
choice but you insist upon
chameleon, one like those
in Savannah's sun
lazing on my deck.

I taught you then *pantoum*
repeating whole lines.
You chose *minnows,* darting
away from hungry nets,
the last line repeating the first,
a form as circular and haunting
as the thought that we
no longer chase chameleons
hiding under hibiscus blooms
and soon we won't net minnows:
you're learning the alphabet
of your body changes,
the growth of each sound,
a vocabulary and language
mine once knew, a Latin
I had to strain to remember as
I taught you then *pantoum.*

Sea Bean Search

for Nicholas at thirteen,
Melbourne Beach, FL
March 21, 2007

Winds froth the waves,
roaring after eastern rain.
Water whips onto shore.

While walking with Fritz,
of matching hair, tousled
blond on brown, frizzled up,

he's ferreted a few keepers:
some wash onto shore
from as far off as Africa.

Hamburger beans, brown
with a darker seam, too hard
for voracious teeth to crack.

Hungry himself and no
sign of girls, he shovels
first a body, arms, hands,

rounded head, Gray Pearls
for eyes, Anchovy Pear nose,
a Red Mangrove mouth

(he can't stop his fingers
maybe it would be a mermaid)
if only he had Moonflowers,

but his two Laurelwood beans
will top the nippled mounds.
As a White Ibis flutters down

to fish, the curved orange bill
a sturdy tool, gouging, digging,
he contemplates his artifice:

two bumpy Blister Pods
the size of English walnuts
or one Red Heart? Neither.

Beachcombers stop to puzzle
at his Yorkie sniffing for crab,
then digging himself into a hole

his hind legs thrashing above
and at the Adamic sand art figure,
its gender obscured by a conch.

Son Slipping Away

Listen hard in the cavernous darkness:
stumble awake from a well-lit dream
into a room whose floor covering you know
but you can't get your bearings, stub a foot
against metal so hard it breaks the big toe;

look for his silver car outside the window
whose cranking sounds must have awakened you;
lean in, shade your eyes, hope that your eyes failed,
were wrong, pray that he and his car aren't gone
for what will you do there, waiting for him alone?

Imagine then squeezing through a pencil passage
within the earth, crawling behind the booted feet
of a spelunker and his single point of light, chest
as heavy as iron, heart rate off the scale, then,
plunging into a bed of bat manure, of cold rancor.

Aftermath
from an empty nest

Now that you're gone,
it's Bach, not rock;
television dark,
books back on the shelf,
no muddy shoes
nor sticky drink dribbles,
towels dry, hung straight.
We eat sitting alone—
correct flatware, elbows down,
not slurping our boring soup.

You left your barefoot tracks
under the dining room table
and just for a moment
I remember little piggy toes
and counting Indians on them—
oh, that skin, sweeter
and fresher than morning—
before I vacuum them away,
returning the house
to its shallow order.

Time
for Nicholas at fourteen;
with gratitude to Brenda and Mills
June, 2008

That day
I'll get off at King's Cross
and you'll go on; perhaps
you'll ride as far as Knightsbridge,
clench your frugal stash at Harrod's
so you can later risk it all on a single
pair of Diesel jeans or Nike shoes. You
might stop at the 'Loo, cross the Thames,
take in a play at the Lyttelton.

When I step off the train without
warning you first, words may fail you,
heart in your throat, as it was at Leicester
when we looked back for your grandfather,
still seated on the train, distracted, looking away.
You could only pound against his back—
Time's winged chariot
then watch him speeding away.
Now, it's your time to lead.
And indeed there will be time. . .

It's your time to read the signposts,
exchange currency, get to "know
your onions" on the roundabouts,
drive on the wrong side of the road,
discover the Yew tree in an Oxford
garden older than Eliot or Marvell
for a hundred decisions and indecisions
before the taking of toast and tea
and how will they cook our eggs
at St. Martin's Café in the Crypt?

I'm still searching the wall map
to try and learn where the line
I'll take will end up—where I'll get off
and who else I'll find there. One
thing I know: there'll be fine things,
things as reliably golden as Big Ben,
as lasting as lapis lazuli, as astonishing
as the windows at King's College Chapel,
as brilliant as the five hundred
karat diamond in the Queen's orb.

There'll be peace, joy, a holiday. *Time.*
I think I'll take a whirl on the yellow line
for one last glimpse of you in the Sherlock Holmes,
recalling The Rupert Brooke in Grantchester.
Stands the Church clock at ten to three?
And is there honey still for tea?
I'll see your tall smile. Together we'll wait
for the signal to cross, look around for a Magnum,
icy and chocolate, the ones we prefer at Tesco's.

Listen, Children

Decoration Day at Phillips Chapel, 2005

Words on the headstones are fading;
Concrete crumbles in a short time.
Four of their babies lie sleeping;
He's next to her in the grassy line.

Concrete crumbles in a short time
The sturdiest silk flowers fade.
He's next to her in the grassy line;
Soon we'll eat lunch in the shade.

The sturdiest silk flowers fade;
Live plants and shrubs are banned.
Soon we'll eat lunch in the shade
As cousins swap lore of this land.

Live plants and shrubs are banned
On the hill where kinfolks reside.
We repeat and remember their lives
Heartsick for them by our sides.

On the hill where kinfolks reside
My name will be chiseled in stone.
Heartsick for them by our sides
We soon must leave to go home.

My name will be chiseled in stone
You will be left to read, waiting.
Don't cry. I won't be there alone;
Words on the headstones are fading.

Women Fleeing Ice

In a field a stream ran by
A-straying from his fellows;
Once a little lad did spy
His face among the billows.
Brief his image fair is seen
In the pretty wavelets green—
Then only weeds and willows.

-C. M. Bellman, "Cradle Song,"
translated by Paul Britten Austin

Why She Came
for Mila and Polina

"No dreams," she said,
massaging my legs with oil
following the sea salt scrub.

"In Russia, no dreams."

I had mine, I was sure,
living one that moment,
reclined at the day spa,
a warmed roll at my neck,
low lights, lulling music,
cracked heels filed as smooth
as a baby's by her strong hands

until her unsettling answer,
this chemist professor fled to
America, trimming toenails.

Alien
for Gillian

A watery wall of homesickness
like a mother's ache for her newborn
rises to Gillian's throat, rises
and knots in memory—
her home, Empangeni,
its stalks of sugar cane,
its orchids and antherium
as profuse as Savannah azaleas,
as familiar as family,

the rose-sweetness
of her mother—
of the dewy garden,
its troweled earthy clumps,

not hard-edged like these boxes
of books she signs for and slices
open, slashing cardboard,
searching as if something were lost
and could be retrieved, unsealed,
some delicious secret uttered
unexpectedly like a just-learned word,
dour, peise, auld lang syne

old words from her mother's tongue,
smooth and satisfying to a lassie,
surrounded by Afrikaans
and Bantu, unclear and harsh.

She thinks she sees a friend
in Checkers pushing a trolley
as fuzzy as faces can scorch
in South Africa's sunshine
and she races to meet her,
but like the sudden snap
of a Christmas cracker,
it reveals the face of a stranger
who puzzles at Gillian's speed

toward her with the grocery cart
past pears, peaches and plums,
at Gillian's shrinking back
as if struck—or stricken,
by a molten piece of the sun
when Gillian remembers
that she is food shopping
far away from home
at the Pig.

Unnatural, all these differences:
Crepe Myrtle for Pride of India,
raisins and sweets in mincemeat,
cars on the right side of the road,
wrong again, she realizes,
fumbling from the passenger side.
She tries to mirror the cutting
edge of the stares on the street
but hers is deflected, dull-edged.

Back at the bookstore,
she draws an Atlas from the box
          and the Equator mocks her.
As she slices into a box
with her exacto knife,
she claws to rappel,
to get beyond the wall, just
to breathe again, to help
the waiting customer,
chatting about the price of lettuce,
the hurricane season,
and aren't the sand gnats awful.

          Steeped in the depths
of his distinct division,
the smug girdler whispers
from the other side of the sun
          le mal du pays,
          cette dommage,
as Gillian grinds her teeth, smiling
at the young, unwitting shopper,
oblivious yet to exile.

The Places I Go

Dead fish and dried turnips
inhabit that prickly place
where I visit each night.

Rest eludes me in settings
that are familiar, the ones
in which I'm still in school.

Final exams are due
and I haven't attended
a single class. I can't find

the schedule. Never have
after night after night
of teetering on the brink

of failure. Or I'm the teacher
and my class won't sit down
wouldn't listen, out of control

while I wait for the principal
before returning to the maze of
a house I own, come back to, visit

which has rambling rooms stock-
piled with antique furniture,
but are all the doors locked

against whatever harm is outside?
I always forget one. Turnip greens
grow untended in a window box.

Last night fish and turtles stuck
in mud in a bucket I watered twice,
then watched them bubble back to life.

November Kitchen

Her kitchen is rosemary.
Pork tenderloin steams her glasses.
A red hot wok sizzles with acorn squash.
Pecan, pear mincemeat, whisper to her;
the oven is heated day and night, ready.
Anise biscotti smells as enticing
as those morning waves swirling sand
when Libby tracked the sea turtle
for Nicholas to her sandy nest
mounded high in early summer.

Wind has erased the tracks. . .
install the Carmen Santiago cd;
sharpen pencils, find lined paper,
practice cursive handwriting;
taekwondo classes.

Besides, conversation is preheated,
wine has corkscrewed their tongues.
He bread ain't done.
The soda in Irish Soda Bread makes it flat.
Nicholas crawls behind a fish platter
on top of the cabinet with his Game Boy
so he can not see Libby cramming
long recipes into her pocket, nibbling
nuts from the pie, dutifully stirring
the pot, untangling her brain.

Bon appetit.
She sits at her customary end.
The crystal kneels on its stems;
napkins unfold in obeisance.
Fragrant green fingers of rosemary,
as pervasive as white sand and sea oats

stalk her at every meal, a seaside of it,
fertile and unfettered. She picks
like a feverish sandpiper
feeding on uncovered eggs.

Going West

Libby's jade is afraid, remembering,
stuffed in and stacked in the back seat
between mops, brooms, and cleaning supplies,
houseplants anchoring this domestic chain.

The shadow of the moving van tows them at sunrise.
Pines drone by like the raspy voice of a smoker.
Brown cows nibble on new pasture weeds.
A sudden patch of purple on the hill is louder
than car horns at rush hour at La Guardia
or early morning clamor in Rockefeller Plaza.

Not that loud, a jolt, as unexpected
as the city worker mopping concrete,
sanitary streets of Manhattan
crisscrossed by despair.
Her daughter would kill for an appointment
with Frederic Faqui in the Chanel Building
but the wind made Libby shrink
walking in this tall cotton.

She waited in line at FAO Schwartz
looking for Pokemon, gotta catch em all.
Her grandson is her Big Eye mirror.
You breaked my dream, he cried,
after the divorce, awakened too soon,
not in his old room. No more moving.
No more musicals; she gets lost
sitting in one seat too long.

Now she rises above the winding road
stretched ahead of her like black ribbon,
il pleure dans mon cœur, levitates.
Her jade is bent like a woman hunched
over a walker; its leaves are the lips
of a child, quivering, about to cry.

Women Fleeing Ice

after an interview of writer and storyteller Kathryn Tucker Windham
by Nancy Anderson in the Monroeville, Alabama, courthouse

As swift as a Spring Pygmy Sculpin
tinier than a crawdad in Coldwater Creek,
Kathryn dunks the microphone in water;
and sips on her trembling falsetto;
she cranks up a wake of laughter

about mean but lovable Billie Jean
whose obituary she had fretted over,
lordy mercy, then in Billie Jean walked,
home from Chicago, simply homesick,
toujours perdrix, she explained, smiling.

As unique as the Orange-nacre Mucket,
as fragile as the Cahaba lily, her species
is without a Latin name, not listed yet
in some Red Data Book, but like all river
life in the Cahaba, endangered.

Nancy casts out questions which bob down
and way up in the balcony, Gerald Chan,
who has treaded water all her life
in Savannah, leans over, whispering
tales of her Chinese laundryman. Listen:

Emma, songbird of Mercer, is hushed,
her lyrics drifting along in his Moon River.
Johnny Mae, born near the May in Blufton,
tells of migrating toward the Pavilion at Tybee,
riding the Victory Drive train under the stars;

the Charleston and the shag, just old dreams now.
She recites a Gullah phrase—last of the *scops*—
as imperiled as singing "Alabama" in school,
as singular as Helen Norris, our poet of laurels.
Who else writes anymore with a pencil,

a yellow number one pencil which, on its own,
is writing her biography? *Ces belles dames,*
illumined voices of our mothers
and grandmothers holding forth,
reminding us that we never had an Ice Age

or glaciers to barb our tardy tongues
or to chip our syllables off short,
to freeze and level our very accents.
Instead we rocked in the shade of our porches,
echoing the rhythm of soft, warm rain.

As starved as an anemic woman,
a woman hungry for rain, we swing
a broad net, circling as far as it will go,
our catch as unlikely as the lure
of the mussel who lays her larvae

in a minnow-like case that mimics
eyes, gills, and scales, hoping
for an unwitting host, some fish to bite
into the bait, dispersing her eggs—hoping
for one to attach itself, glory—to live on.

Crossing Lines

Crossing the near-black line of blue
sea water, divorced women swam
in on wings of wild gobblers
from the deck of the ferry, searching,
on the remote barrier island,
listening for the lost mating call.
Against the northern sky a skeleton
of glory, Lucy Carnegie's mansion,
Dungeness, sits crumbling.

Women struggle with nests for the day—
picnic lunches, coolers, beach towels—
along with twenty-six boy scouts
seeking a badge on Cumberland.
Clustered on the upper deck,
the boys are guided by something
inexplicable until a teenage girl
walks by, already trying to hold
in her own skin at places
it threatens to split.

Libby smirks, her skin as thin
as the cracked ends of conch shells,
her heart as hard as the curving
backs of armadillos, invaders
waddling along the paths where
Lucy's grandfather once drove.
Now in a row set straighter
than beached globs of jellyfish
along the curving shoreline,
the cars are rusting, rotting,
sinking as sawbriars weave
upward, growing green plaits,
eating radiators, rods, and hoses.

Insects and locusts saw steady tunes,
the zizzing of paper over comb,
the chirps, the gobbles, the woosh of waves;
these sounds she came to hear,
no regret at all, she says offhandedly;
she's soaking it up, reflecting.

This illogic nearly works
until she slips up. Her anger
like spiky palmetto fronds
slices and splits any gesture
of any man in words sharper
than a misstep off the path
where undergrowth is so dense
it reveals nature's truth:
wilderness gardened
can be reclaimed.

                    Libby looks
to the horses, a still sculpture
in the dense shade shaped
in the pattern of a pergola—
horses with no bridles, no reins,
no riders, wild, nibbling on sprouts.
She wanders away from the others,
crossing over boxed sand dunes,
a bientôt. Sand spurs lick her legs;
the sun blinds her. A pelican with no eyelids,
she dives for fish, swooping, starving.

Night is Heavier Than Day

1

Even on the summer solstice,
his birthday; he stares
out from their house
which is only half a house
to the yard, a shrunken version
of a yard, telescoped down
like his legs after the surgery.

Worry sets in before sunset,
a nagging, a longing,
for sweet gum leaves to rake,
those spiky balls he used to hate,
for a pool algae-green to treat,
to bleach clear, things he can only
do now at night, so after the cake,
after the song, after two John Wayne
reruns, he lets go
                       his body
connected by plastic tubing
from the abdomen to the pool,
the infested pool that must be
filtered out, dialyzed
by his peritoneum

bloated with fluid, pressure,
a leg cramp bites and holds on
like a snapping terrapin
but he is too drunk with the dream
to stand; he rolls over,
                       then upright.

Winter is worse, its shadows
slipping in as unannounced
as kidney failure, a sudden pall,
obscuring from his upstairs window
the cactus whose needles
are nearly as fine as the one he uses

for Epogen, hormone
artificial and dear that can signal
the bone marrow, such tiny talk,
to produce red blood cells

but nightmare
spills out of the shadows; stalks
toward him, African Milk Plant,
green temple of once arrogant columns
stretched in prickly praise, slumped
with the weight of last night's freeze,
flaccid and humble, an old man's limbs

and he thinks if he had another life,
he would study medicine, nephrology,
just so he could spit in the face
of its objectivity, its jargon

                                    jangles
him awake in a nightsweat,
steaming sheets, pajamas
in the chilly room;
then he changes his mind—
it is a baby he would be,
to feel his mother's cool hand,
to babble back at his grandson,
to understand.

2
His wife had not been able
to separate the seasons,
tensed in her hospital chair;
being herself bent to extremes,
she dreads the in-betweens,
dawn and dusk,
autumn and spring,
as a mother shrinks from unsavory
samenesses in her child.

3

For didn't it happen in spring
and wasn't it backwards?
Signs of death, not new life,
being inside, not in the garden;
holding his hand, not digging;
thinking, too much thinking
yet loving so much
she began to love the idea
of it, or was it fear she felt—
they are so close.

Surely it was night the day
he was free falling, gripping
her like a child frightened
on the first downswing
of the ferris wheel ride,
convinced he was dying.
His saying so over and over:
that was night.

Home with him in autumn,
she could not watch the squirrels,
their flight too gray, too gay,
nor could she write in her journal
for she, herself, might be inked
into the surreal page as she
named such blackness.
What nomenclature
could she use?

She is as confused
as her Christmas Cactus,
too soon bent and nearly split
with its sensual red burden;
too early to plant pansies,
too much to consider
yet their fragile stay,
their roots so easily unearthed
by the greedy squirrels
stockpiling in stealth
as she sleeps, sweet
oppressive escape.

When She Doesn't Understand Something, She Cries

The skate slices the water
like a giant gray lily pad.
Such a clean knifing.
Her laid egg case
hardens, a brown box
nestling under a forest
of kelp fronds and fishes.

Yawning metallic anchovies
gape for food circling the tank
like so many silver wind-up toys.
Clouds of white anemone
stalk the bottom, ready
to wage silent stings
against heavy bullies
in the Monterey Aquarium.

Dr. Detman, voracious
for surgery and science,
was satiated with patients
on seven south, the renal floor.
Charts taped to doors
plotted their daily progress
in the cryptography of medicine
and an intern's scribble,
of numbers and measures.

His patients might hurt
themselves by knowing too much.
This nebulous needle
jabbed them, its point as squishy
as the skin of a sea cucumber.
Some held their hearts
in their hands and cried.

Libby did not cry. When her husband's
transplanted kidney failed, she simply
swam south past his hospital bed
in the river that runs north
toward his brother
who donated the kidney
swimming alongside swift terrapins
that spin tentacles of truths
tangled like the sea green octopus—

Quel est cette languor
qui penetre mon coeur?

truths barking like sea lions
splattered by salt spray;
the rocks spitting it back out,
spilt and spent into the bay.

Fusion

It sucked me first, and now sucks thee,
And in this flea our two bloods mingled be.
                    -John Donne

Blood is one bond; memory, too.
What fuses me to you
if not the codeine-laced dream
in which I was levitating,
floating at will as long as I willed
but should will waver, I'd fall
like the dogwood leaf
wed to its branch
until brilliance browns;
the buckeye's burr,
the hickory nut's hull;
all fall.

Yet Spanish moss clings to the oak,
swings above the marsh linking
river to sea in brackish curves
that seem to sever the two,
but never do; instead shrimp spawn
while flounder flatten
onto their blind belly-sides
until night gigged.

A Dream

Before the scream I was riding
an overgrown tricycle in a skirt.
My patriotic pin was beaded in red.
The ride did not seem dangerous.
Someone had tiny dolls. She said
she had to be able to tell these dolls
apart. To me they looked identical.

I had been looking
in my closet. This event
required orange. I needed a wrap
for my one orange dress. My briefcase
was bulging. A boy was carrying it.
Was I his teacher? The bell
was about to ring.

The scream. I am pressing
against a tightness encircling me,
confining me. I try to break out.
It has me tied down. The weight
is so great I have nothing left
to do but scream. My voice
won't work at first. I try harder
and harder to squeak out just
one sound. Then my husband
calls me. I was screaming,
he said, for my sister.
He wonders why.

Butterflies and Chocolates

Blue Chair butterflies.
They wake and sleep at will.
Up from Aunt Bessie's lap
of knitting they float,
brought with her from Michigan,
brighter than her afghan thread,
one yellow, one red and black.
Someone explains they should
not be tamed, but kept in this wild
state. Suddenly I am birthing
butterflies from my tongue,
no taste, just tiny folded squares
that I blow out like bubbles.
Beautifully varied butterflies
exuding full blown, flying.
Aunt Bessies' needles
keep clicking.

A table of glazed
doughnuts is spread before us
in this doctor's office. Twin babies
in a swing are being examined.
The mother sits in the swing
with the one who has blue-black
markings around one eye
and down the cheek.
A meal entirely of chocolate
delicacies is being served
to a crowd. I find one
already cut open
through its domed top,
thin layer of milk chocolate
rounded like a jellyroll.
Inside is a mint-green mousse
with a sinfully sweet syrup
oozing out from each sliced piece.
Chocolate desserts, chocolate
candy, chocolate everywhere
and a roomful of hungry women.

The Last Page

for Kim and Tim
Wesley Monumental United Methodist Church, Savannah, GA

Shoulders squared, she sits
at a discreet distance from him,
back as straight as his,
dress as black as his jacket,
her head alert; his, keeping time,
their visions twinned
by the notations

but while his hands glide, swooping
and dipping like graceful birds,
hers are folded, brooding in her lap

as he pulls out all stops; then
a brisk move to the edge of the bench,
she half stands, thumb and forefinger
grasping the top corner,
sliding down to the middle,
fingers that know without knowing
the feel of a single sheet;

she waits, unwavering
then flips the whole page, full palm behind
flinging forcefully, her body following,

a form so quick, so confident,
so crisply executed, he
does not miss a beat as she repeats
through five movements of Guilain,
through fugues and preludes,
through the weight of a gothic suite
lightened by the trill of a trio by Bach

and as the last page is turned,
she floats to face us from a chair,
motionless, her hands nesting again
leaving him alone
in his ethereal space
to embrace the standing ovation.

Fruits Of An Age

Such is life upon this earth,
The swift years disappear
First we're born to joy and mirth,
Then laid upon a bier.

-C. M. Bellman, "Cradle Song,"
translated by Paul Britten Austin

Emma's Song

Sing, Emma. Sing mood indigo
while we sip scotch, sing of spring
and old man river, toor-a-loor,
toor-a-lie; your siren songs
brought us, nearly strangers,
together at the Waving Girl,
serpentined us down a street
swarming with bodies, young and green,
too soon weaned from milk to Killian's Red,
writhing like eels, hooked on music
whose sounds shook and tangled them.
We pressed against them
locking shoulders, rugby-style
to stay together.

Sing, Emma, sing,
so we won't smell the urine
draining down from the alleys;
sing of Irish eyes and Danny boy,
it is their day, sing of green
as we dine on riverhouse fare:
Gazpacho, warm; Creole, too spicy
hot; oysters, presided over
until a husband consumes most
of the myth she clings to;
sing, Emma, of hope.

Sing of seven silly women,
make your Memphis boy laugh,
sing as we glide through
the Tennessee waltz;
sing as we clog and kick;
forget your 77 years, and ours,
advancing, too, so that tomorrow
when the electric pink neon necklaces
we sport fade from drizzling rain,
we might, separately, adult
again, hum the same tunes.

Letters
for Sherrie

They always planned to meet.
Girl Scouts. By chance, pen-pals.
Sherrie and Sharon. Weird
the way they both liked barn owls.

Girl Scouts. By chance, pen-pals
sketching in pen and ink for years,
the way they both liked barn owls,
the way they boxed up their fears.

Pen and ink sketched the years,
a Savannah sunset, Texas chili.
The way they boxed up their fears,
they both bit their nails willy-nilly.

A Savannah sunset, Texas chili,
girl talk of high school and college.
They both bit their nails willy-nilly
with up's and down's of marriage.

Girl talk of high school and college,
no thought at all to write of health
with up's and down's of marriage.
Ravenous cells grew in stealth.

No thought at all to write of health.
Unlucky, untimely, dread surprise
as angry cells ballooned in stealth.
Sherrie, haply, was not apprised.

Unlucky, untimely, dread surprise:
no letters from Sharon. O the grief
that Sherrie, haply, was not apprised.
They always planned to meet.

Neighbor

Within the walls of our city
Bob dozes under a live oak,
in his battered lawn chair,
a variety of clay pots circling the tree,
as conspicuous as a camel would be
outside his marsh front villa
bunched up with others
halfway between town and the sea;
something here needles me,
like a name I can almost recall,
something so somehow familiar
I half expect to see watermelons
piled and cooling in that shade.
Bob hears my bicycle coming,
startles, then waves, and allows
how it might rain.

On summer mornings
if there is no one to talk to,
Bob exercises at the pool with Grace.
He figures on how drowning
wouldn't be all that bad.
It seemed mighty pleasant,
according to one man
who'd tried it, weighted down
under all that water,
hard to leave, peaceful and such.
If you tried to stretch out flat, he said,
just as flat as a board on the bottom,
you could find that place
between life and whatever comes after.

Sometimes Bob follows his cane,
tapping out a path along the curbs
of our trimmed and edged lawns.
He waves indiscriminately
at each passerby, every car
within this circular haven

just as my daddy waved, in overalls
that outlasted his cotton fields,
as he walked down Main Street,
Northport, or inside the local mall,
just as he had done on my wedding day,
to Sam Miller and Chappy Pate,
friends from the wood yard,
to his grandkids, to the family-to-be,
as if he were in some grand parade,
proud, as he walked me,
red faced, mortified,
down the interminable aisle.

Gifted they called him,
like the local water witch.
Daddy knew how to dig a grave;
a grave required higher ground.
He sized up the man, or child
shaping a casket shelf of red clay
with only his shovel, worn thin.
He had figured on digging his own,
with his considerable practice—
four for his babies, one
for his wife, two for grown sons,
and too-many-to-count neighbors.

Bob hearkens, stands up
he must hear a crack in my greeting;
his blindness has nothing
to do with his raising,
or trying to rise above it,
must sense something
sliding down my face, salty,
sacred mud, spittle and dust.
Words clot up in my chest
as I pedal off, unbalanced.

Midden of Dreams

In the guest room upstairs
on the top shelf, high
in the closet, a boxed
white satin gown,
its hem properly cleaned
from that one night of dancing.

In the basement filing cabinet
behind the Christmas boxes
near a fully ordered workshop,
letters packaged by decades
stamped with three-cent
stamps up to thirty-nine.

In between a couple
lives a calendared life
among dust-free surfaces,
like the new Dendrobium,
too far away from windows
to wallow in its yellow dreams.

Fruits of an Age

When the clock strikes three
and he asks is it time
for bananas she startled
from afternoon remembering
rises with a slight stagger
to find the fruit.

From the top to the end
again and again
she contemplates the peeling
then steadies his outreached hand
with her own trembling twin.

They seated eat, a respite
from the empty dozing
of interminable hours
from the strain
of the stretching days,
of the days.

Just In Case

Okra and cantaloupe seed
dried and banked
in jelly jars
along with plastic Parkay bowls,
one crammed with Spinner Baits,
a coffee pot that doesn't perk,
a sticky peppermint,
more log than cane
to mix a liquored potion
for sore throats,
aged and flattened bags,
emptied prescription bottles
piled in a basket
with a few forgotten pecans,
oddities squirreled away
cluttering her kitchen,

her nest against
loss, the unknown;
she might plant the garden
next spring; he might
fish for bass.

But it is always a stranger
who cleans a house finally,
puzzling over these stacks
of security, discarding
what she deems useless,
but she will not need
to decide about love;
it does not linger
after the laughter.

Men Who Buy Lunch At The Pig

His eyes are like a flame of fire...
and he has a name inscribed that no one knows but himself...
                                        Revelation 19:12

Jeans raveling over their boots,
shirts hanging out of their jeans,
they wear their names stitched on
for forgetful men who pay their wages,
but one in line is startled when he is called
by name, as if he might have worn
the wrong shirt; then he resumes staring
down past the pocket that names him.

Chicken with potatoes and gravy and peas
scooped into sectioned Styrofoam plates
give-away day-old chocolate chip cookies
quarts of drinks for a gallon-sized thirst
and the essential cordial, two packs of Camels,
please

> *look lady, hurry it up will ya*
> *the others are waiting in the truck*
> *the boss is waiting, and I'm sick*
> *of standing here waiting for you;*
> *you should be the one shoveling dirt,*
> *lady, if you can't figure one simple price*
> *the only way I'm going to have a good day*
> *is to get out of here in time for a smoke*

"Thank you, M'am," he says,
naming her with generic respect,
reaching for his prodigal lunch.

Men Going Fishing

Up before daylight, shaking
younger ones, stretching away sleep,
they convene silently in the kitchen,
buttons and zippers at odds
from dressing in dark bedrooms,
old hair spiked with restless sleep,
as unruly as they had been as teenagers,
as awkward in this kitchen without women
as if they were asking for directions,
admitting somehow they were lost.

Each opens and stares into cabinets,
in separate brown studies, searching,
ripping box tops from cereal,
toasting a bagel or bread, groping
inside the refrigerator for butter,
all making breakfast choices;
some stacking sandwiches to take,
more than enough, just in case,
relatives passing shoulder to shoulder
like strangers shopping for food.

The oldest, an unlikely fisher now,
limps in late hurrying, more eager
to go than his arthritic knees, eager
to repeat tales of how things used to be,
stories the grandsons are too young
to remember, how Gulf Shores
had more fishing boats than tourists,
when there was no limit on red snapper,
grouper, or amberjack and boats groaned
from the reckless gluttony of each catch.

A younger one measures coffee
and sound following his evening
at Live Bait, the lines in his face
        cutting deeper
with each gurgle
        of the thirty-cup pot;
as deliberate in closing a cabinet
as if he were handling fine crystal,
he seeks the simple treasure of a mug;
he knows just where his wife keeps them
at home, but where are they hidden here,
here in this kitchen of moving men?

Dancer Entering a Room
for Martha

Still rose-petal thin, she squeezes in
behind the girl in white tights and tutu.

Girlish bangs, curly hair swept back
from her knowing neck in a severe bun.

Her arms float on an invisible string
or else they are filled with helium.

She draws them down to her side,
singly, and prepares to sit, sullen.

I rise, offering up my cushioned seat.
I want her to *know* I remember

how she used to drift and glide
when she was the prima ballerina

for this annual ball for Russian royalty,
how she could spin in toe shoes.

I want her to kick off the brown low-heeled
pumps, drawing heel to thorny heel

like magnets, making her walk wooden,
her fallen feet positioned for a perfect plié.

The Sleeping Head
after "The Sleeping Head,"
sculpture by Carolyn Watson

Because hers is not,
because she has bolted awake,
fearing creatures that crawl,
she chisels with new fury

focused on finding
in that heaviness of sandstone
layered within its crystals
her own seam of bedrock,

curved into two breasts,
a bust hammer-firm, lumpless,
or a raspy spouse secured
in a house so tightly built

that a lizard could not crawl
through cracks at doors,
splaying his sticky feet and tail
against a squeaky pane,

stunned by her screams,
her sprays of oven cleaner,
her terror to touch the pile
of *Architectural Digest*s

she threw on top of him, unable
to scrutinize his probable demise;
too wary of dark to close her eyes,
she files out the folds of an eyelid.

Icon

for Millie

St. George, his Sankir face
emerging above the swirl
of Vermilion and Umbre chaos,
his robe buttoned in Yellow Oxide
to reflect the heavenly energy
of his gold-leafed halo,
written on birch, tree of life,
art as old as Byzantine,
as sacred there
as the relic to a nun,

with new perspectives, Mildred says,
with the light emanating from darkness
patient and precise layers
applied throughout her daily litany
to her spouse, as persistent as dementia,
as repetitive as a Gregorian chant,
about what she did and why;

yet, compelled, she tried egg tempera
cracking the egg, draining out the white,
cradling the all-fat yolk *much maligned,*
says her tutor, a Russian theologian,
puncturing the lining with a needle
but venerated with purified water,
with Lapis Lazuli and other minerals

to search for that contact point
between human and divine
from dull green through second flesh,
third, fourth—until inner light
exudes, a touch of pure holy white
so that faces become luminous
once they are blessed, like hers, heated
perhaps by the same humbling fire
I feel in mine as I read on his back
how she signed: *Mildred, servant of God.*

As They Wait
for Ray

Leaves of the towering sea grape,
some larger than my palm,
thicker than spreading aloe,
obscure the paved entrance
which faces west.
Long slinky fingers
of a New Zealand spruce
mimic lush banana clusters
near the door of the cottage,
painted as pink as the hibiscus,
tall, with saucer-sized blooms.
Inside two lovers wait.

There they wait for daylight
where the unabashed sun, eager
to strip off her wide skirt,
slides up and brightens
the whole of this endless bolt
of wavy blue-green corduroy,
seamed with dolphins
and a few Right Whales
rickracking a path
back to Nova Scotia,
his last glimpse
of their annual migration.

They wait for the gritty night
holding hands on the sand.
Stargazers, they announce
celestial names as familiar
as his fistful of pills and morphine,
a dark litany for the moon, rising
now more gracefully than the sun.

(Who knows where the pelicans go,
no eyelids against sun or stars?)
They wait for that final light,
As warm and bright as a morning kiss,
as enticing as a slice of the silken moon.

September Ironing: In Memoriam
Jewell Smith, August 2, 1904-September 9, 1993
buried September, 11, 1993

One early morning horror brought back
another, and that one triggering more,
too much for hands to sit and watch all day.
I began ironing clothes from a laundry rack
run rampant with summer cottons, just in time
to pack them away, hangers stretching
above the length of the sink, the basket
on the dryer bulging with clean linens
from family gatherings, yellow and green
picnics, white Sunday dinners, lace napkins,
blue tablecloths under favorite soups
at supper, bubbling, steaming up. . .

                           you were born
the same year as the Iron Man, forged
for the World's Fair, Vulcan set on top
of Red Mountain until he rusted, cracked
and was dismantled for repairs, laid down
in separate pieces on the ground and you,
buried eight years ago today.

Today I counted napkins, smoothing,
folding, folding and smoothing
into stacks, first the gingham, then plaid
but only nine of that kind, three missing
from the whole . . .

                           a rot gnawed
a hole from a bedsore into your hip. I
was the child with your fiery temper, the one
who could stamp my feet in front of you
and have my way, but not that day. I
willed you to rise from your frilly rest,
put on your overalls, and get to the red

field, call me to come pull corn and I
would run, this time I would not whine
and balk, let me try it again.
                              I screamed for you
to get out to the barn; George
needs at least one new shoe.
Look at my sole; it needs a repair.
Not a soul is left who knows
how to use the shoe last.
Time for you to wake up, Daddy.
Where is that little grin when you
tickled me under the chin to wake me?
Wake up. We'll go walk at the mall
and you can wave at everyone
who calls you Farmer and we'll get
a Dr. Pepper afterwards, I'll say
not too much ice, you never
wanted a lot of ice, I hate
this ice that has cracked Vulcan,
that I feel on your skin

burning mine all day,
this day when Absence
loomed like a starched tablecloth,
not with spray from a can, but stiff,
the old starch we cooked—everywhere,
everywhere—tops of twin towers,
doors, floors, hands, arms, fingers
holes in buildings bigger than
my emptied laundry room, too many
to count, to remember, too much
to fold and store away. For what
closet or chest could ever contain
such magnitude, such loss.

Posed, 1948

for Clyde Stanley Duncan
September 28, 1947- August 1, 2007

The sun-bleached porch
of the Worth McGee place:
you would be one in the fall
and I had just turned six.
We were seated in a rocker
caned with white oak strips,
soaked and woven, one piece
of Mama's necessary art.
Claudy, two, stood by me
with his arms folded.
My nephews. We three
and Cecil McGee,
our Lone Ranger,
guarding us with a cap gun
in his scabbard slung
around his overalls;
he must have been five.

We all were as clean
as a pan of spring water
and a wash rag could
make us. My ruffled sleeve
from a guano sack stood out,
starched, ironed with a flatiron
heated on the wood stove;
your tiny tucks and pleats
were flour-sack white next
to my print and the satin ribbon
I have imagined to be yellow
pinned into my blondish hair.

Four pairs of bare feet—
who had summer shoes?
Four pairs of dubious eyes;
four curious faces, but
not one hint of a smile,
not even for the funny faces
behind the photographer.

Before, we were happily playing
in the dirt under the shade tree,
cracking a few black walnuts
that had fallen prematurely
minding our 'cropper lives

until they placed us in a row
on the spot that had been piled high
in cotton the month you were born,
the soft, fuzzy playground on which
I broke out my two front teeth.
Did your mother get the chair?
Who smoothed our hair?
You were placed upon my lap
but didn't they notice the walnut half
in Claudy's hand, and the black stains
tattooed on my mouth and right thumb
just before the snap of the camera?

Your nubile hands had never
picked a chinquapin; never grabbed
a spring lizard; never been pricked
by a cotton boll, or fired back china
berries from a wooden slingshot
when caps were shot at you.

This week we walked into your green
garden of melons and tomatoes
watered by the well you'd witched,
unmindful of the summer drought.
You pushed back large leaves
with your walking cane,
uncovering cantaloupe nearly
ripe, and clustered watermelons
as close as sleeping brothers.
Lush tomato vines drooped
with reddening fruit, all
fertilized with fish heads
and bones you've filleted.
You've strung your plot
with electric wire against
deer, armadillo, and raccoons.

Your natural Santa beard
shimmered in the sun,
protection of another kind.
You've become Santa.
You can't hide your grin
when it tickles a child
whispering into your ear
her tender Christmas wishes
as parents year after year
record this holiday scene.

Year round your cheer
has routed out the scourge
of a deserter father, the fall
that killed your stepdad,
flashbacks of a country
whose white rabbits haunted you,
the shock of the divorce
that robbed you of your children,
and a mother's untimely death
by the very disease you have

yet, there we sit, posed,
my arms around your waist,
my tiny dead-bolt lock,
childish and defenseless now.

The Dogs of Death

on the painting at the Speed Museum "The Interior of the New Church in Delft
with the Tomb of William the Silent" by Cornelius de Man.
(William was assassinated.)

There is no object so foul that intense light will not make beautiful.
                                        -Ralph Waldo Emerson

Light obscures the newly dug grave,
its dark mound of dirt unnoticed,
a penny dropped by a curious
tourist, one of the breaths of a day.

Except for white spots, the two dogs
in the foreground might be shadings
of brown and black, as normal as night

until our own assassin comes stalking,
throwing light over that part of the canvas,
compelling us into the nave, up marbled
columns, to statuary rising up, up
to orange flags, waving allegiance,

but too late. The light hangs heavy there,
the music of the organ magnified,
its sounds stopped, then drifting down
to the wheelbarrow, dark as the pit.

The dogs nose the black cracks
between green and white floor tiles,
sniffing for the scent of red.

Kitchen Psalter

Tiny Carl shall so reflect,
Seeing pretty flow'rs have deck'd
The springtime of the year.

-C. M. Bellman, "Cradle Song,"
translated by Paul Britten Austin

Possessions

The dogwoods
just beyond the fence
were mine, I thought
and the mimosas
and pines,
for I had claimed
them from my kitchen
window as I wrote,
a measure
for my seasons.

Today a machine
felled my gauge
stripped the hill
to dirt
and I wonder
without its bonnet
of blossoms
white and pink
and its coat
of pollened pine,
how will I know
Spring?

Consider This Lily

. . . he shall blossom like the lily; he shall strike root like the forests of Lebanon. His shoots shall spread out; his beauty shall be like the olive tree and his fragrance like that of Lebanon. . .

Hosea 14: 5b-6

A filament as fragile
as an umbrella for honeybees,
topped with a dusting of yellow,
its anther. Six male stamen, purest
white on white pie-shaped petals,
encircle the pistil female parts,
standing tall, curved but stable,
the Cahaba Lily, perfect and rare,
at home mostly by the side of rivers.

Far from its moist beginnings,
its cluster of two silky blossoms
and two slender buds on a stalk
grace a spot in my garden bed,
a summer muck of dried daylily stems,
a ground tangle of briars and weeds,
one small dead dogwood, sprouted
too close under the oak tree. Daunting,
but I begin weeding around the lily.

Perhaps I could not salvage the rest,
but this unexpected gift—like a child
after the famine of infertility—
must be preserved, kept whole, safe.
I set aside my pruning shears and gloves,
searching for supplies of sanctuary:
a bucket upside down, pew to sit, and sate
my eyes, my brain, my very fingertips,
as if I were writing an icon on birch.

I clutched and curled the charcoal pencil.
No artist would be so clumsy, so bound
to capture the tortuous leaning stem,
the slender cascade of four elongated leaves.
But my motivation was clear: each
blossom is brief, or so I'd read,
would last only a day like the hibiscus.
I would construct an image, a tabernacle
on paper to be shaded later inside.

Pastels would brighten my smudgings
etch the image like a baby's palm in plaster,
so that tomorrow if I walk outside to find
its papery petals limp, fallen, or folding
back upon themselves, ripped by winds,
fringed with brown worry, I can consider
this confident lily, flowering, its leaves
unfurled, more striking than a Ginger Lily,
if less fragrant, brief, and less strong.

Kitchen Psalter

I ache to Celtic sounds,
when I bake a Fruity Flan,
or Pear Mincemeat Pie,

but I twang to Hank Williams
at my sister's house cutting
okra or scraping corn.

No music at the other's
so we muddy the stillness
with our discursion of kin,

who's died, the new baby's
name and what a crying shame
we don't harmonize more often,

fried apple pies or sweet potato,
Mama's winter pies
I'm reminded of all summer.

A pie in my oven, Mutsu apple,
bubbles with a dusting of nutmeg,
her very thumbprint—

nutmeg, nutmeg—worry
the dough. Its name evokes
her hands, the twin of mine.

I crush new sage, the herb
she grew and dried for seasoning
pork sausage. I inhale its essence,

hungry for hymns, craving
"Come Ye Sinners" as she
baked and hummed. Amen.

Sisters

Shucking and silking
done, we bend over
a stainless steel sink,
side by side by side
scraping sweet kernels
down the cob
or up,
Silver Queen,
twenty-five dozen ears
to be frozen
for our winter tables.

A butcher knife,
older than the oldest one,
fits her hand. We defer.
The other takes a sharper
knife. I take potluck, last
in this assembly line.
We cut down the cob,
raking off little white knobs,
scraping the row,
milk squirting
like squeezed lemon.

Each immersed in her own close
commerce, we do not discuss
dementia, two-pack-a-day habits
or what we feed addictive genes.
For there is work, work.
We only argue tiny matters:
did Mama cut up the cob
and scrape,
or down?

Mantra

Cranberry-apple conserve,
pear mincemeat: fruit jars
ringed with rubber tips,
inched from their boiling bath,
cooling, clicking, sealing.
A sterile vacuum.
Canned. Conclusive.

Firm berries, apples,
or greenish pears, washed
peeled, stirred, and simmered,
sugar and spices, measured,
and sometimes a song.
Then cooling, clicking, sealing—
a formula I want to preserve

like crunching through oak leaves,
giggling a pumpkin from the patch,
arguing the right-sized tree,
licking sugar cookie fingers—
the way we did
before depression
bittered our bucolic.

I hum now past the dread,
even out the knots in my voice,
to quell the uncertainty in yours
and contemplate
the promise of repetition,
of cooling, clicking, sealing.

Eating Dirt

The smell first tempted her
to taste red dirt from high
on the steep bank sprinkled
and steamy with spring rain
as she skipped home
from the school bus.
Her daughter craves
the stench of angel dust.

Last year she thinned her lilies,
sniffed a handful of humus
and threw it into the holes
we dug in my crybaby clay.
Not one grain of grit
between my toes—splash
water over my bare feet;
never on my teeth—rinse,
rinse, rinse the lettuce,
spinach and turnip greens.

Our oldest sister has sandy beds
like Mama's yard scratched
clean with a brush broom,
packed down like brown sugar,
as absolute as planting beans
on a full moon, or Good Friday.
Unschooled on crank, crack,
or methamphetamine,
like Mama, she weeds out
"dope and strong drink."

Our humus, sand, and clay,
as inseparable as blood—loam.
We can't remember who rooted
the Confederate Rose, whose hand
sowed the Queen Anne's Lace,
who sprouted the English Dogwood.

We plow and pulverize and puzzle
what to do about crab grass
and the niece in jail
who calls collect.

I give it over to the lilies
as I dig twenty-six more holes,
ignoring the sticky clumps,
shoveling in sand
from my surer sister.

Bursts of orange and yellow,
of frilly purples and pinks
from last spring's humus
rainbow my kitchen window
while a streak of green salves
the throats of the lilies
as they rise and fall freely,
unchoked by familial winds.

Scuppernong Jelly

It's that time:
September
my old nemesis

when a muggy hush
falls each day
with temperatures

a crow's caw
from the pine
is intensified

when my fall harvest
has dwindled to
greenish-gold grapes

smashed, cooked,
bubbling up hard
in clear juice,

to be strained
through cheesecloth.
Scalded jars

wait to the side.
Filling, cooling,
skimming, sealing.

It's that time,
phlegmatic, slow,
sticky sweet.

Sacred Seasons: *Carpe Diem*

Now that summer's dog days
and Labor Day are packed away,
picking and shelling pinkeyed peas
is only a young, hot memory.

Fueled by spring's lettuces,
its allure of baby scallions,
and first new turnip greens;
we hungered to gather them.

Those we would imbibe
with relish and abandon;
a drunk's morning drink,
those we could not hold in a jar.

Now we scrounge for the last
of the pears for mincemeat
or chutney, eager to preserve
more than one winter requires.

Jars of tomatoes and beans,
squash and pickled okra,
corn, lima beans, and chowchow;
fig, peach, and apple preserves

color and crowd our pantry shelves
until we finally grow weary
with this prodigious industry,
appetites as dulled as a plow

point when crops are laid by.
So we dig, dig the sweet potatoes,
shell, shell the dried butterbeans,
wait for the frost on the collards

as the season fizzles out
like old baking powder.
We conjure up Christmas citrus,
hunger for crisp pastels of Easter.

A jar of scuppernong jelly held up
to the morning light is cloudy;
such failures of cheesecloth
and other measured efforts

make it clear to me that I
for one am done with this litany
unless winter changes my mind,
its sudden ice, our stilled hands.

My Back Porch, August

August 20, 2005

> Dogged days.
> Sun and rain and rain and sun
> yellow the older basil leaves,
> purple the stalks with blooms,
> nurturing new green nubs,
> nubile country girls
> unschooled yet in the seasons.
> Last year's rosemary, doused
> and resurrected by rain,
> blankets its hidden pot.
> Thyme froths up
> like pistachio pudding.
>
> The rickrack plant has sprouted
> caterpillar's legs, and climbs
> the wall and window.
> The waist-high jade,
> no longer afraid, stretches
> its weighty limbs of water
> balloons and some drop.
> Blue and white heads
> of plumbago and begonia
> frizzle from daily dampness.
>
> Brown spots polka dot
> the smaller jades.
> Christmas cactuses
> snap at crucial chain links.
> The light, white-green aloe
> fans out, an onion sliced to bloom.
> The root bound exotic plant
> shaded in a dry corner
> sports new toothy fronds
> after its spring buzz cut.
> Maidenhair ferns are wavy

in the heavy heat, permed.
One scheflera is tree-sized;
the miniature is lopsided
with happy children's hands.
The purple vine cascades
over its hanging basket
in grapelike clusters.

       I'm hungry
to preserve this profusion
before fall's dehydration,
before winter's icy fingers
strangle the song of crickets,
the cacophony of tree frogs,
choking out their drone,
my summer's white noise
against grief, waiting inside.

My Back Porch, November

Bird feeders hang empty of jays and wrens
no hungry sparrows or finches; no Indigo
Bunting, but I expected him to go south.
Today even the redbirds couple elsewhere.

Chipmunks and squirrels, foragers
once furious for any vagrant seeds
are sleek now with acorns, hickory
nuts, and posh persimmons,
holed up and napping, slowed

by this silence which has fallen
like drifting leaves in quiet homage
to age—

begonias gone leggy; plumbago
scarcely blooming, scraggly; impatiens
just hanging on; basil, a stalk of pith;
mint, browned. Only the jade
stays plumped, succulent,

enviable. It is so quiet here that I think
if I listen hard enough, I could hear
leaves whispering, a voice
like my mother's calling for me.

My Back Porch, Late November
for Tommy

Twenty-eight degrees
according to his inside-
outside thermometer
and the porch is empty,
stripped of its foliage
the way a church is purged
on Maundy Thursday,
and rooms made plain
after the tropes of Christmas.
Two cushioned armchairs
wait, stark, their rattan arms
brittle with cold, cushions
faded and damp. Wrought
iron green doesn't make up
for my leafy curtain, mostly
tattered and brown, lying
in heaps on the ground,
or for his voracious voice.
The only thing stirring
is a flock of blackbirds
fleshing out a skinny oak

the way he leavens
my kitchen. Their chirping
is boisterous like his laugh,
as abrupt as the skewed lives
he outlines for me from the news.
Stories steam up over his coffee,
creamy and sweet, antithesis
of my black cup gone cold,
of my botanical cocoon.

In the Sweet, By and By. . .

My sisters put up beans and corn,
peas and okra, tomatoes and squash;
they preserve anything growing fresh
with the diligence and ardor of the ant.

This year at one sitting we peeled,
sliced, and preserved fifty pounds
of unnamed pears, the canning kind,
I learned, in the shade of Ann's water oak.

The process so nebulous it must be art,
no science was ever this inexact;
Ree said watch for a change
in the bubbles, *wait for itsy bitsy bubbles.*

*Didn't you ever watch Daddy
making syrup?* Ann figured quickly
I was too young to have helped with that.
That's how I learned, and watching Mama.

*If you make pear preserves
till the day you die, you won't have
one batch turn out the same,* she assured
later when I phoned for some formula.

I had fifty pounds of Keiffers
and fifty pounds of Pineapple Pears,
bought from a farmer who named them.
For a week I reeled off recipe names...

Pear Preserves, Pear Conserve,
Pear Jam, Pear Chutney,
Pear Mincemeat, Pear Syrup,
Pickled Pears, Pears *en Framboise.* . .

The morning after a batch was sealed,
I stood and stared as I pasted labels,
a thing my sisters have never done—
no need, they know what is what.

The rich pinkness of the syrup,
its viscosity near perfection,
barely moving when cold;
the curves of the whole pear halves...

working so hard, wondering why,
remembering other summers,
remembering Mama, the pioneer,
the dog days when she died;

Daddy followed another September
as politely as if she'd called, having lost
his little smile long before, his farm
gone; now, his second wife, too;

wondering whether to plant a tulip tree
for Len, who gave up our girls quartet
to lie under shady oaks, leaving us
shorthanded in song and story

and Lonnie who chose a sunnier spot,
the truest farmer of us all, a giant
himself, growing head-high collards
and five-pound sweet potatoes

and William, sweet William,
crazy for redbones and rotgut,
but running two miles for Mama,
when she hemorrhaged, for a ride

and the four babies I never knew
buried by Mama and Daddy.
This is all too much to preserve
in a jelly jar, in a week. . .

so industry, as it will, takes over
as I peel pears, slice pears,
cook and stir pears, watching
bubbles grow small.

The Dance

on the occasion of an organ concert,
September 18, 2005 2:00 p.m.
by Richard Phillips

1

Hands like butterflies,
lighting, touching,
stroking ivory keys,
sipping a prelude
by Buxetude, building
to a fanfare staggering
with its speed and breadth
while underneath, feet—
feet, feet,—waltzing,
swinging to steps
on the pedal board.

Toccato in F major:
he prances with his back
facing us, his feet, trains
patterned on velvet tracks,
powered from above,
marionettes dressed
in ballerina shoes
and strung with invisible
thread. I hold my breath
hoping his footwork
will not tangle, or crash.

2

Mary Bea first mesmerized me
with her graduation recital stops
and afterwards agreed to play
the wedding march for me
on a piano which I learned
too late was a pitiful plug.

Today while others hummed
the tune of "Danny Boy,"
its older lyrics came back to me:
"Londonderry Air," the way I sang it
shoulder to shoulder as she played,
as I had trilled in junior high chorus.

Would God I were the tender apple blossom
that floats and falls from off the twisted bough...

3
The carved and swirly
wood of Miss Alma's organ,
as strong and straightforward
as her tall, slender carriage
when she married my dad,
filled their tiny front room.

Each black laced brogan
primed separate pumps
bellowing out notes
without tall pipes
to accompany
the roomful of kin
all singing the hymns
of amazing grace,
her voice the high,
high soprano lead
as we followed,
watching her faithful feet
etched into worn patterns
of her meager soles.

Just as I am and waiting not
to rid my soul of one dark blot...

Bid me rise up, then,
welcome, pardon, cleanse
dancing, dancing
I come, I come.

About the Author

Kathleen Thompson was born in the northwest part of Tuscaloosa County just off the Mormon Road that leads to Phillips Chapel Freewill Baptist Church where she will be buried alongside her daddy, Jewell Smith, and her mother Tempie Savannah Taylor Smith. Her daddy used to tell the story that James Claude "Doc" Guin, Sr., came to the house that day (Monkey Sanford's birthday, too, her oldest sister always adds—because the siblings were sent to his party to wait) and asked Jewell's permission for his son, J. C., to deliver Tempie's tenth baby. J. C. needed the practice: it was his first delivery.

Taught in sixth grade by G. W. Hatchett, 1953-54, at Etteca School, Kathleen still treasures her notebook from his class. The students copied twenty-one poetry classics from the blackboard and were required to memorize one of them. The spiraled wire is rusted now and the careful pencil penmanship fading, but Kathleen can still recite most of those poems.

A former teacher of high school English with a BS from the University of Alabama, Kathleen is a graduate of the MFA in Writing program at Spalding University. She has published poetry and prose in various magazines and journals. Her short story "Living Like the Lilies" was selected for the anthology from Livingston Press, *Climbing Mt. Cheaha: Emerging Alabama Writers*. Most recently "Nothin' to Cry About" was published in *REAL: Regarding Arts & Letter*, and "Mother and Child," in an anthology from Excalibur Press, *Christmas Is A Season!2008*.

She has two published chapbooks of poetry: *Searching for Ambergris*, Pudding House Publications, and *The Nights, The Days*, Negative Capability. She was named The Alabama State Poetry Society 2005 Poet of the Year. Currently she is a "Road Scholar" for Alabama Humanities Foundation, 2007- 09.

She writes children's picture books, children's poems, essays, articles, short stories, novels, and sacksful of letters and e-mails.

Cover Art: Detail from "The Sleeping Head," acrylic and ink on board, by Carolyn Watson. Watson holds an MA in Fine Arts from Louisiana State University.